miss lost nation

ANHINGA PRESS

miss lost nation

Bethany Schultz Hurst

2013 Robert Dana-Anhinga
Prize for Poetry

Selected by
Richard Blanco

ANHINGA PRESS
TALLAHASSEE, FLORIDA 2014

Cover art: Photograph "Old Gas Stove,"
          Sergej Razvodovskij/shutterstock.com
Author photo: Tagen Baker
Design, production, and cover design: Jay Snodgrass
Type styles: titles set in Myriad Pro, text set in Minion Pro

Library of Congress Cataloging-in-Publication Data
Miss Lost Nation by Bethany Schultz Hurst — First Edition
ISBN — 978-1-934695-39-5
Library of Congress Cataloging Card Number — 2014939479

Anhinga Press Inc. is a nonprofit corporation dedicated wholly to the
publication and appreciation of fine poetry and other literary genres.

For personal orders, catalogs, and information, write to:

ANHINGA PRESS
P.O. Box 3665 • Tallahassee, Florida 32315
Website: www.anhinga.org • Email: info@anhinga.org

Published in the United States by Anhinga Press
Tallahassee, Florida • First Edition, 2014

Contents

III.

Acknowledgments

Grateful acknowledgment is made to journals in which these poems originally appeared:

5am: "Networks of Crumbling Mines"
Cimarron Review: "Preordained" and "Problems with Nudity"
The Cortland Review: "A Sturdy House"
Crab Orchard Review: "Dust Bowl, 1936" and "Settler"
Gargoyle: "The Unlikely Event of a Water Landing"
The Gettysburg Review: "Complications of a Late Freeze" and
    "Every Couple Before Us"
Kalliope: "For George Washington's Mother at the Start of Each
    New War"
New Ohio Review: "Crisis on Infinite Earths: Issues 1–12"
Rattle: "Sweet and Golden Soup"
RHINO: "Elegy for Beauty School and Fallen Satellites"
River Styx: "Disarmament" and "Homesteading"
Sixth Finch: "Search Party, Called Off"
Smartish Pace: "Water Line"
Spoon River Review: "The Truth, in Utah"
Valparaiso Poetry Review: "Ice Cave: Shoshone, Idaho"

Thank you to Adam Hurst, Wayne and Suzanne Schultz, and the rest of my family for their support. Thank you to my colleagues and teachers, especially Jonathan Johnson and Christopher Howell, for their guidance. Thank you to judge Richard Blanco for selecting my work. Thank you to Jay Snodgrass, Lynne Knight, Kristine Snodgrass, and Rick Campbell, who have taken such good care of me and my work and have made me feel so welcome at Anhinga Press. And many, many thanks to Greg Nicholl and Susan Goslee for their friendship and for their indefatigable work on the manuscript; without them this book would not exist.

miss lost nation

I.

For George Washington's Mother
at the Start of Each New War

She surveys the damage to the orchard.
Grim-lipped, tasting lost tarts and pies
and cherry wine, she grabs a wedge, an axe.
Fashions a crude wooden boy from the felled
tree: stiff peg legs, round knotted eyes. It never
sprouts twigs under its arms; at night
it never awakes wide-eyed, startled at sap
oozing from its crotch. It never hefts
an axe, utters *I could never tell a lie.*
The stripped branches are still flowering white.
The wood seems always to stay green. Even later,
when home is dark and cold and her son
miles away, teeth chattering as they wait
to sink into some substantial word, it will not burn.

Tourist

There's a reflection of a fat white man
in my photograph of the Rosetta Stone,
his belly annexing hieroglyphics, Demotic, Greek
as if his girth were another language whose code
we've been unable to crack until now. He is among
those who enter the inner shrine to robe the gods.
I'd thought the stone would be smaller,
easily held in the palm, like something
from the bottom of a cereal box or
a keychain souvenir, which is an example
of how my low expectations allow for moments
of awe. The stone is big, big enough for Ptolemy's lineage
being a god sprung from a god and goddess
in three languages and now the fat man, too,
the wrinkles in his shirt artifacts of a tightly packed suitcase,
reminding me that I was only one in the crowd
at the British Museum, no matter what my photos pretend,
and this stone was broken and brought here, too,
along with shards of the Sphinx's beard,
mummies dragged out of their homes in the bog,
hands covering their eyes and skulls still grinning
because they have to. But the stone
wears the fat man like a diaphanous gown
and in the small view from my camera screen, it's not
his fault or mine and what else could we have done?
There's something else to be decoded here.
If you broke open my body, it would surrender alphabet
until all that's left is what I was in the fragile beginning,
before my tongue had cleaved itself to language,
when my parents' indistinct voices murmuring
in the next room clothed me.

Minimum Wage State

Which is kinder: to wave back at the man
dressed like a giant taco or to ignore him?
You know, the guy handing out coupons.
I'm uncomfortable with the outfit.
During tax season, an accountant in town
pays a woman to play the Statue of Liberty
and in green robes and spiky crown
she stumbles up and down the sidewalk,
in all kinds of cruel weather. When I see her,
I have a hundred questions and not one
is if that accountant should do my taxes.
I'm not sure if the lady is all there.
She would be easy to write off. Saying
"not all there" is a euphemism, which is
putting what we think is gross in nicer
clothes. Still we fidget when it passes,
like that brief period in junior high
when I sat with the Special Education
kids at lunch because I wanted to look nice.
Then someone called me *retard*, and I saw
how open the borders were. So I crossed
the cafeteria to where I couldn't be mistaken
and sat near the huddle of popular tables
in the uniform right jeans and no one talked
much to me. It was hard work. I could
barely eat. O Giant Taco, O Lady Liberty,
forgive me if I throw away your flier
no matter how much it might save me.

Ice Cave: Shoshone, Idaho

The parking lot is empty, save the looming statue
of a thirty-foot Indian and the sound of a car door
closing. Decades ago, to fit more tourists,

they blasted the cave entrance, let in too much air.
The ice melted. Now that hole's been bricked
and a door keeps the cold in place. In the high-desert

half-mile from parking lot to cave, chipped concrete
prehistoric people are the only figures. The last
of the tribe. The squatting woman grips a stone

between her legs and grinds it against another
stone. The man's hands are shaped to grasp
some spear or staff that has long since vanished.

This is what they do forever, landmarks
where even rivers slip underground. Two years ago,
Christmas, a car slid into a snow bank down the road.

The children's pictures were front page
the next day, when the girl's body was found.
The father had stayed behind with the car,

let the children set out to their mother's, ten miles
away in the storm. They made snow angels at first.
In court, the father struck his head against the table

while a lawyer defended *we all put our children*
at risk, toss our babies in the air and expect
to catch them. Behind the door to the cave, ice

is building another frozen lump in the desert's gut.
A gift shop vintage postcard depicts a girl ice-skating
in the cave "even if outside the temperature reads 100."

She has cut faint trails into the ice. Her scarf is
spun out behind her perfect frozen pirouette.
At the cave entrance, the concrete woman grinds

her stones and the tour guide tells the story
of an Indian Princess preserved inside. But it was only
a few years ago the cave thawed out and nobody emerged.

Sweet and Golden Soup

Fifty-six people have jumped off from the same lamppost
on the Golden Gate Bridge. It must be secretly marked
safehouse or *tell hard luck story here* as if the bay
could be cajoled to offer up some scrap it's been
withholding all this time. I crossed that expanse
in a ferry when I was a child on a family vacation.
I didn't think then about how many bodies
were beneath us. Earlier I'd shoplifted
for the first time. I thought I'd swiped
a sugar packet, but found out on the ferry's deck
it was silica beads. *Do Not Eat.* I had no idea
what silica was except a disappointment and
a sorry start to a life of crime. We were headed back
from Alcatraz. Later a street mime thought
my sister was pretty, escaped his glass box to give her
one imagined flower after another. My mother
pointed out hidden flaws in beautiful women
to give me hope for the future. Freckles, overbite.
O how I dreamed the Most Crooked Street
would be my home. But there was nothing secret
about that postcard-obvious gash. Cars lined up
to traffic its perfect turns. Even when no one was looking
my sister clutched her make-believe bouquet.
My hand closed around my pocket's worthless contraband.
In Chinatown, plucked chickens illuminated windows.
Dim sum and wonton were unopened gifts.
If I could read the restaurant names, one would say
Here is the place, here is a sweet and golden soup
that will ensure you are never hungry again,
but my parents thought they said *dangerous neighborhood*
so we went back to the hotel and had hamburgers.
On the way, my mother pointed out homeless people

by pretending they didn't exist. Then I shared a bed with my sister
and remembered the cityscape from the ferry's deck,
how from that distance I thought I might hold the city
in the flat of my hand or crush it between my fingers
to extract some kind of juice, bitter or sweet.

The Unlikely Event of a Water Landing

In one frame of the safety card,
passengers slip out of the plane
onto a rubbery yellow slide. Then,
a baby bobs along in his special life vest,
dangling long and articulate limbs
under the waterline. He more resembles
a small and bald adult, scale and proportion
ignored, as in a medieval painting where
newborn Christ is mature and huge
on Mary's lap. With no setting
or vanishing point, descending planes
can be left out of the picture. At least
you don't have to worry this is a real
disaster, the infant floating alone against
an empty sky, or about what happens
outside the frame. If any child
could save himself, it's this one.
His illustrated legs look capable
of wading safely through the breakers
onto some island we've imagined. This baby
could scale a palm tree, crack open a coconut,
sip some milk and search for the horizon,
wait for anything else that might be chosen
to crawl out from the ocean and
onto this blank shore.

Infinite, Separate Houses

It's stupid I want to save this potato chip
because it looks like Abraham Lincoln.
I won't even look at my cereal:
Each bran flake could be a president
or saint. People often get their bearded men
confused. The lilacs are blooming again
and politicians are trying to convince me
that Jesus would prefer their tax plan.
The best way to claim what isn't yours
is to pretend that it's your destiny
to have it. It worked for the settlers
when they railroaded their way west.
But I'm glad I didn't like the paint color
"Indian Tears" when we remodeled
the bathroom. I paused over ten shades
named for flowers before settling on
"Eternity," which makes a toilet
seem a lot more important than it is.
The trash can I wheel to the curb
is filled with what I've determined
worthless. Saving that potato chip
would be the wrong sort of tribute,
but I can't eat it, either. A dark train
might still be passing in the distance, carrying
a corpse through overgrown battlefields
and cities budding with houses. *We cannot
consecrate — we cannot hallow —
this ground,* Lincoln said at Gettysburg,
because it was not our rightful place,
because it was sacred already.

Homesteading

In the old West, you drew a line in the dust and presto,
you conjured up a home. You moved cattle anyplace
you wanted if you had enough rope. It was a song.
Get along little doggies. With your ear to the ground,

you could tell if the lawman's horse was coming.
In 1982 in my backyard sandbox, all I got was an earful of dirt
and a rumble that turned out to be the garbage truck
collecting our trash at the curb. Oh well. It's not like

not using a napkin would turn it back into a tree.
At the dinner table, my mother sang *Happy Trails*
like Dale Evans to trick us into eating quicker. I never sang
a solo. Too much tremolo, the choir teacher said,

so I played a shrub in the school play. Not much
could hang from my short branches. Masking tape
marked where I stood on the stage. In the wings,
third graders waited, dressed like Indians

in faux leather vests, which seemed like another
kind of trick. I didn't have any lines. In the old
West, someone was always gunning for someone
else's stuff. There weren't many courtrooms

if they caught you, but there were lots of trees
and rope. After the play, it was hard to find our car
in the line-up of other similar cars. I dropped
my paper leaves in the parking lot. I became

a tumbleweed. My mom thought I was littering.
I was humming *this land is my land*.

The Last Undeveloped Land

His mother is getting over pneumonia
and still smoking. I say, "There's nothing
worth slaving over anymore. This vacuum,
for instance, who's to say it even works?
When I went to prom I had a ten p.m. curfew,
look where that got me. I hung dead roses
in my room for years. Later when the phone
never rang, I dreamt of boys in T-shirts
that read I RESORT TO LONG LAPSES OF SILENCE.
They were intentional. The boys came around later
when I'd stopped thinking of them. We kissed
behind the hospital in a Colorado wheat field,
the last bit of prairie still in view of the mountains."

Proletariat

From TV you learned Soviets wore fuzzy hats
shaped like Kremlin domes. Americans
should've worn skyscrapers, strip malls.
Maybe that's why you liked hair spray
so much. At the Olympics, the Soviet anthem
was like playing "The Star-Spangled Banner"
slower and backward on a record player
in hopes of finding an encrypted message
back when you had time for that sort of thing
and your bedroom was a country of its own.
Princess phone, pedicure. You blacked your own eyes
with shadow and outlined your lips like a thick
crayon drawing. In geography, you traced
the shapes of countries, the USSR vaguely like us
but askew and the jut of Texas melted off.
You'd thought puzzle pieces should snap
together, a record dragged backward
against its spindle should yield an answer,
but there was no big picture, no indication
of where to dig for the disposed tsar's bones.
The record player lid latched down like a
dirty bomb. Your bathrobe was a trench coat,
the belt wrapped three times around you
gawkily. From cartoons, you learned Natasha
could've been sexy under her coat in amoral,
slinky dresses, but was all conniving angles
and overdrawn face. You were supposed
to root for the moose, who won despite clumsiness
as if fate engineered his success. His antlers waggled
above cowlicked fur in a way that said *dumb*.
Their shape was so complicated, though,
you thought they had to stand for something.

A Sturdy House

The wind throws itself at the house over and over.
I used to be like that too, but slashing someone's tires
ain't gonna make him love you again. *Make me,*
I'd say when my mother requested the tedious,
forgetting that she already had: for ninth months
she made my mouth and ears, determined
the perfect ratio between the length
of my fourth and second fingers, fingers named
for doing what any other could do, like wear a ring
or point. Just as I suppose any other lump of cells
in my mother's body could have borne my name,
but it still wouldn't have done the dishes when she asked
or believed in the invisible things that she did.
The wind has a face that I imagined, though the house
isn't changed for withstanding it. The next morning
I check for loose shingles, a splintered door,
but already the house has forgotten
all but its own foundation.

Every Couple Before Us

This is a love story: It turned out
the tattooed man and the bearded woman

were just mannequins doctored with sharpie
and fake hair. What did I expect? No freak

would work for a 50-cent show. You could still see
the perfect mouth behind the mannequin's beard.

Such defacement seemed both shameful and
deserved, especially since I was sixteen.

I was there with David, whose pregnant girlfriend
was too embarrassed to go out. I thought of her

just once in a funhouse mirror. The realest thing
was the two-headed piglet in formaldehyde,

and I couldn't tell if it had actually been born or not,
or which way would be worse. I was glad

I wasn't the one who had to choose. I was sick
with fried dough and cigarettes. We passed

the booth where lost kids were supposed to go
to find their families. Then we found the main

attraction, the Ferris wheel, grinding against the sky.
When we were suspended at the top like every couple

before us, I realized David's leg was touching mine
as if we were fused. The houses below looked so small

only broken people could have fit inside. Then the wheel
resumed its lurch and reminded me that I'd be dropped off

later, too, at one of those houses, and on the way back down
I wondered who got their money's worth.

Disarmament

From across the rancher's field,
a junked-out tractor watched us
like some adult who'd given up
on caring. Sledgehammers had already
convinced the access hatch to open,
so we stole underground into the old
missile silos, armed with flashlights.
The unstable light caught KEEP OUT
but was unable to conjure a whole
picture out of darkness. The boys
lit cigarettes. Me, I'd swallow any pill;
nothing that small could touch me.
I barely bought that I held pinprick eggs
suspended inside. In the silos, giant bodies
of cold war computers were split
into empty chassis, their thick bundles
of cords cut, buttons still labeled
under graffiti on the front: CONTROL,
POWER, LAUNCH. Later when the boys
cut the flashlights, you couldn't tell
how close a body was until it touched you.
I braced myself. We strained against
buttons that kept us from going too far.
Down there it didn't matter. I wanted to go
further. We were full of ourselves,
atoms fat with disaster. If we could find
something untouched, we'd be the first
to trash it. The missile bay was empty,
so I dropped a penny. I never heard it
land. I didn't think then I might have fallen.
What waited at the bottom? It was the future
when we climbed back out. I felt diminished

in the open field. The coin I'd dropped
was still plummeting underground and
the rest of our lives spread out before us
in the prairie grass, which pretended nothing
happened underneath. The tractor, still
standing sentinel for one side or another,
could have been a casualty. But after years
of work, it had just been left there
to rust into a half-life. If I could have found
the single bolt still holding it together,
I would have ruined it for good.

Preordained

When I mispronounce a word, I suspect
that's the Lord telling me not to use it again.
Hush. Not meant for you. I drag seaweed
to the desert, searching for a new way
to say *home*, having eliminated entire
vocabularies. When I dig for the foundation,
sand reclaims the hole. I'm no carpenter.
I build no walls. No windows. Or maybe
my house is one giant window
that I can't close. Is it strange that seagulls
fly through the living room? Maybe they were sent
to clean the carpets. They feast on crickets
and caterpillars. A butterfly protests
we're a part of a plan, but we can't all
come from cocoons. Falling asleep in one form
and bursting from the sheets in another
doesn't run in my family. As a girl, I'd say *help*
and it sounded like *hope*. Everyone laughed.
At the shore, I said I wanted to be a mermaid,
and my sisters wrapped a towel around my legs,
bound it with rope, and tossed me in the sea.
When I sank I spoke to the watery light
of the in between and wondered if I'd surface.
I was resentful. They knew what I meant.

Atomic Woman

I.   Kit

I'd tried to prepare. I packed a toothbrush. Hygiene products. Then there was this flash, broadcast on the horizon. Who wouldn't want to watch? All the girls who ducked and covered, kept themselves intact.

I'd packed photos of family so I could find them again. There was still a space for something in my kit, but I couldn't decide what I'd need.

Utility knife?

An extra set of keys?

Afterward, I suspect this body's not a safe container. It doesn't even feel like me.

I feel bigger than myself. Like a girl who could do anything. Who would.

A manual can opener.

My tea length dress becomes a mini-skirt.

I hit the road.

II.   Fall-out

For a while I crush girls prettier than me, consort with ruined skyscrapers.

Now I'm just asking for directions, but the tiny men seem alarmed. The tallest thing around, I'm picking up strange signals. I can't make out the words, but I can hum the tune. All this paper I have is worthless. No one recognizes the faces printed on them. There has to be something I can exchange for what I need. Everyone keeps looking at my gigantic chubby knees.

In a burned-out forest, I unpack my kit. I'm looking for something to put it back the way it was before. Who is the baby in this picture? I kind of recognize the cropped-out person holding the baby before her. What happened before *that* photo was taken?

When I try to repack, nothing seems to fit. There are all these extra pieces.

III.   Shelter

When I find my way home, Mother is in the basement. She cracks open the door. Tinned meat lines the shelves. I tell her all the bad things I did were just the names of rock and roll bands. The Staying Out All Nights. The Taking What You Wants. The Everything Buts. She doesn't believe me. Neither of us is used to me looking down to her. She is disappointed. She wants to let me in, but I can't squeeze through that bomb shelter door. I hope she has a way to open all of those cans.

Sleepover

Those nights the floor became a body
writhing with sleeping bags and blond hair.
Julie, Julie, Ashlee. We whispered about a girl
our age found in only her underwear,
murdered at the reservoir's edge. I was terrified
the parents might hear us talking. It broke
the contract. We pretended all houses
were the same, but that was not my father
sleeping in the next room. I couldn't bear to look
in the bathroom mirror when we chanted *Bloody Mary*
three times. Which Mary did we even want? Maybe
a different one each time. Some queen. A virgin, a mother.
The moms brought us bowls of chips, and the dads
seemed lost when they wandered into the living room,
surprised somehow that they were dads.
I never slept. I zippered myself into a sleeping bag
bearing the outlined body of a cartoon princess.
That was a refrigerator humming in the kitchen
but it had a different pitch. Outside the yard flooded
with black shapes that had been swingsets and trees,
and beyond that waves and waves of houses, and inside them
you couldn't tell what kind of people were sleeping. Now
those squares of light were bedroom windows
and not just light itself. The bed pushed up
against an opposite wall. The light switch
not where you'd expect.

Water Line

The first rain washed the marker epitaph from the two-by-two,
and the cross itself vanished after a winter under snowdrifts

like the time you dropped an oar from the rowboat
in the flooded dell. You came back when the water dried

but the oar was gone. You thought it had been resurrected;
in another world something rowed in circles,

tracing your name. You didn't realize layers of mud
and muck become a resting place; your dog Sam

was still in the pasture even if his marker was not.
Years later, you left behind the new dog for college

where that summer Spring Creek, too full and fast
to remain itself, devastated its banks and then the city.

Your then boyfriend called you to describe the man
who clung to the telephone pole and then slipped away

into the water before a choice could be made, how to save him.
Afterward, the university library's card catalog

still named the ruined books, call number: FLOOD,
like a fixed point in the stacks, a place to retrieve

what's not admitted lost. The basement interred books
warped with fat pages, as if they held something so true

they couldn't bear to close. You called then-boyfriend
less. After disaster, you might as well rename it all,

each animal pair descending the ark. The library stacks
were punctuated with gaps. The lights turned automatically off

when your time was deemed enough. You were in the dark
before you could even start. It became an excuse. Now

your fiancé says *keep your name when you marry*,
but that's just something snagged in the net

and not what you're really after. You return
to a dog-eared page and can't remember why.

The underlined passage doesn't speak to you now.
In hushed pairs, the wedding party proceeds.

Your veil trolls the air faithfully behind you and again
in the recessional, though something should be different now.

You're a boat, listing to one side. You're waiting
for replacements. You're carried across the threshold

of the new house. Water climbs the porch stairs.
It has poured over the foothills into the pasture,

erasing any landmark, and creeps up
your dress's train. This is your job, to remember

where you buried them, and to give each dog
the same reliable name: Sam, Sam, Sam.

II.

Miss Lost Nation

After she tucked you in bed and turned out the lights,
your mother's face seemed gone forever.
But just because someone left the room doesn't mean

they're dead. My father grew up in Lost Nation. We have
no one there now. Miss Iowa 1986
grew up there, too. For decades her face weathered

on a billboard reading *We Love Darcy*, and I did
love her even if I'd never met her because
I'd been in the same café where she'd eaten

pork tenderloin sandwiches. I practiced smiling
just like her. Later, I met her cousin, who told me
Darcy married and divorced, then found work

modeling her hands. They took down the billboard
a couple years ago. We moved out west. I'm the last
with the family name. Just before he died,

I drove my grandfather around Lost Nation's
square-mile farms and he told me the names of people
I didn't know who used to live there. But the old silos

and schoolhouses weren't there anymore
to mark corners and we got lost on the way back
to the rest home. Still, every tree was a story.

When we finally returned, he greeted the oak
on the nursing home lawn as one he'd climbed
as a child and picnicked beneath. It seemed

convenient. No one knows for sure
how Lost Nation was named. In one story,
an immigrant was searching for his family,

who'd left the old country before him.
He wandered into the green valley, asking
if anyone had seen his lost nation.

That's where the story ends. You never know
if he found them. So what's the point?
You can't pick up what you weren't there to hold

in the first place. Instead of family trees,
I read magazines, study the ads for dish soap
and Vaseline. Just above the soft hands, I imagine

there's a face I remember and beyond that a curtain,
and on the other side of that, a room filled with people
whose names I know and they will be so happy

when I step out onto that stage and find them again.

Dust Bowl, 1936

Your skinny leather purse coughs up
a nickel. You're ushered into the dark

where you could be someone or
no one's mother. Then the grainy film:

tractors rolling over the horizon like tanks.
They almost drive themselves, anyone

could hold that easy wheel. These
are the plows that broke the plains.

But miles from water, the furrowed lines
can't bear, no matter how hard-scratched.

Now the dirt collects. It is the only thing that sticks
to the ribs of cows. A persistent guest

that sifts inside the houses. You don't
know who's invited to the table,

but you scoot closer. Newsreel music
swells. On his dusty plate, a boy draws

a box with thick walls nothing
could trespass. Is this a perfect

house, one not blown through
and filled with something else?

One that locks what is suffering inside?
Still your stomach rumbles.

You can't see who's filming, but of course
someone is in charge. The next shot

is rigged, the cow skull moved to cast
a longer shadow. But that doesn't change

that the cow has starved. The close-up
child's face on screen is lit harsh and

gaunt. In your hands, would it shape
to something softer? What could you

afford? You could use a drink
inside the movie house. The cracks

begin to show in your dry skin.
You can't recall if someone

has been sitting in the empty seat
beside you. The reel keeps spinning

around its hollow core, and dust motes
line up in the projector beam

as if waiting for some direction.

To a Prison Escapee in Search of New Clothes

The whites on the clothesline surrender.
But that's not a real gun. Just a carved-soap
dummy. Shoe polish blackens the wrist
of your prison-issue suit. With each flap
of a shirt in the wind, you vanish
and then return. Funny how the hollow
of a gun makes it real, gives the bullet
a chamber where it can live. I know. I too
have dreamed of cakes that weren't really
cakes, but smuggled something sharp
and hard beneath their mounds of icing.
And the sandwich I'm still hungry for
is the plastic toy I gnawed on as a girl,
an isosceles triangle skirted by viridian
lettuce ruffles. I knew the exact flavor
it would yield when finally I bit through
that brittle form. Trust me, if I thought
a bedsheet rope would get me anywhere,
I'd be knotting it right now. But instead
I hang the linens, display their stains
shaped like states where I will never go,
and would I want to anyhow, knowing
that those uncertain borders were made
by sex and sweat? Go ahead, strip the line.
Just leave me with that chunk of soap
whose form you willed into escape.

Elegy for Open Windows

The roll of toilet paper hung backward
on its spindle may be a signal of distress.
In college, too poor for Harvard,
Richard Nixon delivered groceries
before dawn, so no one would see
the sweat drip from his brow to the boxes
cradled in his arms. Contempt breeds
carefully, like pedigrees. Later,
his homely smile ached in blue-lit TV rooms.
When, instead of scandal, he spoke of Checkers,
his cocker spaniel, men retreated
with newspapers to bathrooms.
Behind shut doors, voices couldn't carry.
Then the women closed the windows, too,
to keep light, like bruised fruit,
from spilling to the street.

Purple Heart

I have never been this sad before, I say
when my soufflé falls or the leaves or your arm
once around my waist in brief and heartbreaking
orbit of my foreign body. Be careful
with the oven door. Your body flushes
in knowledge of words like *exit wound,* and mine
in sorrow of dirty clothes, or a burner
on for hours before I remember. How cold
the floorboards as I return to the kitchen
just in time. Before a bee stung me once,
I'd gotten the verb wrong: *I've never been bit,*
I'd say, but even one sting allows the body
to learn the difference. A bullet passes both
perfect understanding and irrevocably between us.

[the stunt that killed my double]

I.   The Stunt

The stunt that killed my double
has been cut. It was the tasteful

choice, but we've lost
continuity. In one scene my shoes

are black, then red, then
black again. The editor can't stop

touching up the film. I didn't know
the double's name. I try

not to get attached. After the accident
I had an urge to take

her glittering shoes, but of course
I have a pair just like them,

only nicer.

II.   Eulogy

I'd admired my double for doing what I wouldn't. Then once on
location, I stumbled into her trailer instead of mine. Snapshots of
dirty children framed the mirror. Unclean clothes stretched out the
smiley faces on Walmart bags. A litter of Monster cans lolled around
with their push-tab mouths open. I wanted to correct their grammar.
Her vodka wasn't even good.

After my double died, her whole trailer was lifted up and carried away.
I never saw where it ended up. I swear someone keeps moving mine.

III.   According to Wikipedia, Dangerous Stunts
        My Double Survived:

leaping off a cliff into raging waters

climbing the entire height of a skyscraper without wires or nets then
dangled from a broken clock face

using four hungry crocodiles as stepping stones across a river

breaking off from a conga line formed at a skating rink, bursting
through the fire exit and on to a hellish journey through the city streets,
dodging buses and cars, ducking under semitrucks and crashing into a
baby shop.

                                                        It was a house
that did her in.

IV.   Funeral

Everyone did a double take when I flung open the door to the chapel.
I was late, had sat through most of the wrong service next door. My
double's relatives were in jean shorts and ratty t shirts. They tucked
trinkets in her arms, made the coffin a discount bin. Each time I
peered inside it was a different scene. Now she's holding a pink angel
figurine. Wait, was she wearing a trucker hat earlier? Wardrobe must
have reclaimed her shoes. Her left sock had a small hole. In the parking
lot, her step-siblings sprawled across the hoods of souped-up pick-up
trucks and squabbled about what she would have wanted. They hushed
up when I walked by. I was pleased.

Wait, did they think I was the good one, or the bad?

V.   The Stunt

Take Two. We're over budget.
They said do my own stunts or

hit the road, but I can think of no place
like home. Well, you can't say

I don't have pluck! Yesterday,
a burst of flame and smoke

caught my coat but the burns
aren't anywhere that show.

My co-star can't breathe
through his cheap mask,

so we gave him a straw. Today
is the big stunt. If I stand

right where they tell me
when the house front falls,

I'll be saved by the open window.
I keep thinking that after the dust

settles, it'll be like waking from
some crazy dream and I'll finally

recognize who was there all along
underneath their makeup. Action.

I'll just tighten this buckle. I'll give
this scene everything I've got, but no one

is taking my shoes.

Problems with Nudity

It's cold. You bruise. Scabs
embroider your body with the wrong
message. At the department store,
hangers screech along their metal racks,
dressing and undressing empty space
in a way that reminds you of the week
you spent inside your apartment
with no words left for the world and so
you pulled the curtains back and forth
on the rod, out of boredom at first
and then earnestly, an alphabet emerging
from the degree and speed of each tug
and then a grammar and syntax until
you were telling the man outside on the bench
feeding the pigeons what appeared to be
from your window a tunafish sandwich
your entire life story starting at age six
when you stood at the mailbox
lifting your dress for passing cars, and ending
at that very moment when you invented
a new language by stripping a window of its view.
The man outside nodded, threw bread
to the pavement in a generous arc
you both understood. Then you said, *Open
close close open. Open. Open.*

Later, I Was Dropped with Indifference

Last night in a dream I mistook Johnny Mathis
for Stevie Wonder, and if you don't know
who they are, you just need to know this:
that's wrong. Hence *mistook*. I've also plucked
the wrong cloak from the coathook, loved it
at once, that red hood against my face.
And I've always been aware of the present tense.
That's why I was a virgin. The lone flat stone
retained in the palm while others scuttled across
the lake. I was held close. I mistook lovers
for my grandmother. Woodcutters
rescued me constantly. I never returned
the cloak. I was a stone. Or a fossil.
A piece of broken glass worn smooth by water.

Upon Being Tied to the Railroad Tracks

I don't believe you're a villain.
You'll cut me loose before the train.

I hear it chugging somewhere
in the distant desert flats, straining

to pull its dangerous load. There's weird
acoustics out here. Too much space,

like an empty stage. A mouse coughs and
it sounds like dynamite. Or the other way

around. We used to drive out to the plains
and smoke in dry creekbeds by the trestles

of a bridge we thought was haunted by Indians
drumming for war. The beat was so steady

it was hard to believe. We found out
later it was a pumpjack a mile away,

pistoning for oil, its sound trapped
beneath the clouds. That Indian massacre

we thought of actually happened
two hundred miles south.

Why would we want it any closer?
Let's say it never happened. No, let's

say, let's say something that makes it
make sense. Say that rumbling sound,

the puffing smoke on the horizon,
the railcars filled with weeping

explosives are too far away to matter.
A long fuse that loses its spark. Say

you're not the villain. It's this rope?
The track? Whatever's fueling

the train? Here: you say something
that makes me believe the train

won't ever come, and I'll just
lie here and forgive you.

Elegy for Esther Williams, the Bathing Beauty

There was blue light breaking
in waves over her body. Her skin
unwrinkled under the weight
of water. In parlors, men dreamed

her above smoking jackets
and ottomans. When they caught
her luminous waist with their arms,
she vanished. She fluttered.

Her well-choreographed breast strokes
wove among us who declare:
We are empathetic. We understand
the weight of human sadness.

Moon Landing, Faked

I was used to this kind of production.

I was a star.

An elaborate suit held my body hostage. It looked better that way.

Behind my visor, I clenched a pencil in my teeth so my face would think I was smiling.

It was a trick my mother taught me.

Fishing line reeled me toward the ceiling when I took a step. Union workers held the line somewhere. I was overexposed, couldn't see beyond the bright stage lights. But the union workers were overpaid. I just knew it.

For whatever camera, I took off my helmet and cradled it. I showed there was nothing up my astronaut sleeves. Then I produced photographic evidence of slain terrorists.

I bit harder on my pencil. I was getting queasy.

I fished around in my helmet for a while. Grainy footage: one magic bullet, two bodies, one pink pillbox hat. I was looking for something else.

The real will that said I'd finally get what I deserved.

I believed my mother was still watching.

You couldn't fool me.

Inside my empty stomach I could hide all sorts of props.

That birth certificate was faked.

I grinned full of splintered pencil.

Back inside my space capsule I began to saw myself in half.

III.

Reruns of Old Westerns

I.   *Broken Arrow*

The rusted bones of broken-down pickups
seem indigenous to the west, but they're not.
It's not regional to shunt a pile of useless stuff
into some field you can forget. You've forgotten
things all over the map. Your nightgown
hangs from a cactus arm, lipstick rolls down
an empty theatre aisle, a corsage pin
sticks itself to a church pew in Pennsylvania.
Following your truck down a single-track road
is a plume of dust ever-widening, like coyotes
spilling down the Rockies and Appalachians,
over fences into eastern cities they shouldn't know.
You know how to feel at home, too, when you're not,
how to creep into an unfamiliar crook. The domestic
don't stand a chance. They stake something they love
in the yard and are left with frayed rope in the morning.

II.   *Have Gun, Will Travel*

Wanted posters listed AKAs like actors' names
on a movie marquee. When one name wore out
you made another. There used to be that kind of room
to forget in the West. Then we forgot not to kill
so many buffalo and then we forgot how sad
that is. It became a fact and not a new penny
to turn over and over. You pocketed it deep
or spent it in the Dallas airport toward the purchase
of a souvenir shotglass emblazoned with a single star.
That city was all air conditioning and the insides
of hotels and cabs, though your mind played reruns

of strong horses and lassos that put strays back
in their place. You expected bleached cow skulls,
though they're not native to the West. Cows die
everywhere. Over those bones, coyotes always snuffle.
We tried to kill the coyotes, too, but that didn't go as well.
Only the alpha is supposed to breed, but shoot her
and all the betas take her place, pups roil
in every belly until there's no more room
to hold them in the West where they belong.

III.   *Gray Ghost*

You sneaked out of the hotel bed and left the shotglass
and the West. Now you watch the Atlantic both cast up
ancient driftwood and erase its own shore. When the tide goes out,
you want to gather, not forget. You put the smoothest shells
inside your mouth, envy that idea of home, one that is your body.
Imagine the beta's bewilderment when she is suddenly fertile,
more than a sack of slack bones on the pack's edge,
raising the alpha's pups. Would part of you want to be left
in the field, bones poking through patchy fur in announcement
of what your body couldn't hold? You forgot to count how many
months it's been and you're so hungry you could eat
a horse. The sky is an open mouth howling. You become
an echo. Then you forget you mimic, become only a sound.
You've pushed yourself to the farthest shore and what
you thought had settled in you pitches up against your skin.

Upon Return from an Ice-Climbing Trip

"I look fat in these pants," I said. "In fact,
I look pregnant." He said, "What's a matter,
don't you like babies?" I like babies fine.
They are better than rocks or chipped tea cups.
The baby in my dream, for instance, squirms
red in my lap until it finally hovers
inches from my peaceful arms. But that's not
the point. The point is some people
live their whole lives like this, convinced
the mountains are a spine emerging
from something greater, suspended
from sheets of ice and rock in hopes
of touching that soft and yielding body.

Birds, Disappearing

Last spring at the Catholic church, they found
the outline of a bird etched on a window,
glass splintering where the wings had spread
like flames. But there was no blood or feathers,
no light bones crumpled at the sill. It was a miracle
and then the same thing happened at the Lutheran
church down the street. No one took note.
It had been done. Still, that summer birds
exploded in my mind. Those mornings
I awoke to my room on fire for ten minutes:
cut tulips in the vase burning from within.
I worried about bodies, how to touch them,
where they go. If they're just cast out
into the weeds. It's November now and sunlight
has slunk around the south wall, tired of me,
my arrangements of dried leaves. I trace
the patterns of migrating geese. Over and over
they drive a wedge into the sky. It is raining
broken glass. I count every fallen thing.

Settler

Even the tumbleweed
  is a stowaway sneaked in
    with the grass seed, given

an easier-to-say name. It became
  American. We are lonely
    when it stumbles by, but it's just

a weed. We made it
  a thing sadder than itself,
    like a nursing home lunch.

Small portions cut up already.
  Showdown: who will swallow
    the pastel pills measured out

into a tiny paper cup? The tumbleweed
  is a lump in the prairie's throat.
    We could have named it

torch or parasol, but now
  it's just what's leftover
    from the blossom. A new

resident is rolled up
  to the table. They all end up
    here: caught up in a fence

wherever they've been blown. They can't
name how many million
scattered seeds. Instead

they remember the purple bloom
before they broke away.
We hear them rasp

in foreign accents. Then they are sticks
that say nothing at all.

Our Ideas of Ghosts

My oldest sister says she feels like a ghoul, going through the family
linens in the farmhouse attic. I just want that apron with the
embroidered peacock to be mine. My little nieces slip tablecloths
over their heads and sing-song *ooooo ooooo*, their idea of ghosts.
Mother sighs. Moths have either tatted lace from boring fabric or
eaten holes in crocheted edges. I'm either a favorite daughter or no
daughter at all. I've eyed the family portraits to see who's tallest.
Though my sister says she's five-five, I'd give her five-three, tops.
There are gaps between our smiling faces. My sister leans over
my shoulder to teach me to knit, takes my hands as hers. I can cast on
forever. Are ghosts woven from discarded things? All day my sister
tells me who I was before my memories of who I was. It's like trying
to squeeze into old baby clothes. When I was a child, the craft store
gave out yardsticks to help us remember their name. My sisters wore
ours down to a splintered ruler so I'm no good at measuring now.
For instance this scarf I'm knitting never heard of straight lines and
curls back in on itself. *That's normal*, my sister assures me. I stitch
and stitch but it never grows. I haven't learned to cast off. I can't
imagine the tiny crooked body this could warm. *Who do you love
more?* my older niece asks and I can't confess, but I'm afraid I might
like knitting better than purling because I learned it first. At night
everyone shares the first floor beds. I'm put in the attic. I tell them
that's okay. I listen to the scratch and burrow of squirrels in the eaves.
I'm not afraid of ghosts. Still, something might be touching that
broken doll, or unpacking the boxes I consider mine. In the morning,
we reinter the linens we don't want and exhume the heirloom silver.
Mother assigns it to our middle sister, the one who couldn't make it
back to the farm, who didn't appear in this poem until now.

Crisis on Infinite Earths: Issues 1–12

I.

I'm at a poetry convention and wish I were at Comic Con. Everyone is wearing boring T-shirts.

When I give the lady my name, she prints it wrong onto the name tag. I spell it and she gets it wrong again. Let's be honest: it's still my fault.

II.

Japanese tsunami debris
is starting to wash up
on the Pacific shore. At first,
they trace back the soccer balls,

motorcycles, return them
to their owners. That won't last.
There are millions more tons.
Good news for beachcombers,

begins one news article.

III.

In the 30s, William Moulton Marston invented the polygraph and also Wonder Woman. She had her own lie detector, a Lasso of Truth. She could squeeze the truth right out of anyone.

Then things got confusing for superheroes. The Universe accordioned out into a Multiverse. Too many writers penned conflicting origin stories. Super strengths came and went. Sometimes Wonder Woman held the Lasso of Truth, and sometimes she was just holding an ordinary rope.

IV.

Grandma was doing the dishes
when a cockatiel flew in the open window
and landed on her shoulder.
This was after the wildfire

took a bunch of houses.
Maybe the bird was a refugee,
but it shat everywhere
and nipped. She tried a while

to find to whom it belonged,
finally gave it away.
Then she found out
it was worth $800.

V.

Yeah, so there are a lot of birds
in poems these days.
So what? When I get nervous
I like to think of their bones,

so hollow not even pity or
regret is stashed inside,
their bones like some kind
of invisible-making machine.

VI.

Is that black lab loping down the street the one someone called for all
last night?

Phae-ton, *Ja*-cob, *An*-gel, or *Ra*-chel, depending on how near or far
the man dopplered to my window.

VII.

I can't decide which is more truthful, to say *I'm sorry* or *that's too bad.*

VIII.

One family is living in a trailer
next to their burned-out house.
It looks like they are having fun
gathered around the campfire.

The chimney still stands
like something that doesn't
know when to lay down.
Each driveway on the street

displays an address on a
large cardboard swath, since
there's nowhere else to post
the numbers. It's too soon

for me to be driving by like this.

IX.

Crisis on Infinite Earths (1985) cleared up 50 years of DC comic inconsistency, undid the messy idea of the Multiverse. It took 12 issues to contain the disaster. Then surviving superheroes, like Wonder Woman, re-launched with a better idea of who they were. The dead stayed dead.

Now the Universe is divided neatly into pre and post-Crisis.

X.

I confess stupid things I'm sorry for:

- saying that mean thing about that nice teacher
- farting in a swimming pool
- in graduate school telling everyone how delicious blueberry-flavored coffee from 7-11 was
- posing for photographs next to beached tsunami debris.

How didn't I know everyone liked shade-grown fair-trade organic?

XI.

I wish I could spin around so fast that when I stopped, I'd have a new name.

XII.

Here's a corner section
of a house washed up
on the shore, walls still
nailed together. Some bottles,

intact, are nesting inside.
I wasn't expecting this: ordinary
things. To be able to smell
someone else's cherry-flavored

cough syrup. There is
no rope strong enough
to put this back together.
To escape meltdown

at Fukushima-1, starfish
and algae have hitched rides.
They are invasive. What if
they are radioactive? Thank

goodness for the seagulls,
coming to peck out
everything's eyes.

Networks of Crumbling Mines

The mine swallowed its workers weeks ago,
and still on car windows and gas station doors
handwritten notes chant *God Bless Our Six.*
Elsewhere, other people die every day
but we hear nothing of it here.
It doesn't rank high on the list of letters
children write, distant tragedy being just that.
Distant. So noose that ribbon round a tree rather than
your neck. Speak only when death strikes close,
offer your throat in hopes that it won't
bite. What else is there? Look taller, make noise,
run like hell? You can't when you're on fire.
In the mines, it's always burning.
They put pipes to the surface to vent the heat
and build the city regardless.

Bathsheba, Submerged

From your palace roof, you spied
on the woman undressing
to bathe. I can't stop watching

when the deep water
oil plume unfurls into
its season-long bloom.

In the springtime the king
should be with his men
at war, but you stayed

behind. That sludgy flower
metastasizes unchecked
for months. You stuck

the husband in the front lines,
then comforted the wife,
undressed her for yourself.

Now the surface glistens.
Months later, you didn't
want that baby. Then when

it got sick, you didn't want
that baby to die. But you
got over it. You asked

Wherefore should I
fast? Can I bring him
back again? I get being

practical. I have places
to go. I have to keep on
driving. At the station,

though, I gnash and moan,
wrangle uncooperative
coiling hose. I fill it up, transform

my guilt into spectacle. When
you finally stepped outside
the palace, there was a war

and starving women argued
over whose child should be
eaten first. You had no child left

but ripped out your hair anyway,
as if that helped. Watch this: I rent
my blouse. I don't enter

my preferred customer
number. I am better because
I mourn. I would pay more

to stop myself from looking
at that picture of the pelican
sludge-heavy, oil slick,

as slippery as a silk.
Underneath I wear
a sackcloth. I'll make

sure that you are watching
when I finally peel it off.
I'll use it to swaddle

whatever I snag along
the shore. My dark hair
will blossom. I'll disappear

when I step into the water.

Elegy for Beauty School and Fallen Satellites

It's not even *beauty school* anymore, but
cosmetology, which has nothing
to do with the cosmos. Maybe
the mannequin heads, housed in shag wigs,
are dreaming of scissors, the blades
coming together and then apart,
a movement as big as celestial bodies
re-entering atmosphere. An
interruption. Years ago, I asked
my grade school teacher how to spell *interrupt*.
Don't worry about that now,
she replied, and still I stumble over r's,
transpose letters until I'm left with *interpret*.
Don't worry about that now, the way
the mannequin's eyelashes flutter translates
into satellites and angels. Maybe they are
dreaming of scissors: the snip, snip
of air, the shearing of empty space
around their smooth faces. Some things fall
and don't get swept into neat piles.

Complications of a Late Freeze

I.

The ground is frozen when my friend speaks
of playing Chopin, the complicated
phrasing and the long stretch of fingers
across keys like a perfect body he knows
without wooing. Nearby, the crocuses
are shocked from showing too soon.
I can tell only of Chopin playing
in the emergency room, the car accident
I had at sixteen, and the beautiful boy
on the sidewalk who'd caused me to swerve.
This is the wrong thing to say.
I have no scars. When I was a child
and not hungry, my mother would say,
There are starving children in China.
That was wrong, too.

II.

I have no scars. Only my fingers are blue
with cold, the color of the veined hands
of a man I overheard at the diner.
He said to his wife, *It's supposed to thaw*
Thursday, as he pushed his pork chop
across the plate, *but we can't wait*
that long to bury him.

Neither Here nor There

And the yellowed cornstalks around us
were bending in the wind because
they were bending in the wind.
They rustled like things
I've decided were sad. It's not
that the sky cares or doesn't.
It was hard to know
what to listen to on the radio
when I drove, headlights on,
in the procession.
Sometimes irony isn't right
and neither is sincerity:
the town was named Lost Nation.
I ate Jell-O at the reception lunch
and I don't know how
to feel about that.

The Truth, in Utah

I should let you know
there was a layover. First
we circled the great swirls
of Salt Lake reaching pink
under thin ice and salt crust.
I was hungry for warm bread
the entire flight, for the oily skin
of salmon crackling on my tongue.
I was hungry and a handful of pretzels
was nothing. Years ago, I dreamed
that the words that would save me
were chalked on a cracked sidewalk,
the jumbled letters just short
of becoming clear. As we touched
briefly down in Salt Lake, I saw weeds
in the alkaline soil between chunks
of pavement. By the time
I finally reach home, luggage grafted
to my shoulders, scraping ice
from my car — this is unbearable.
I should tell you the truth:
in Utah, the runway unbuttoned
its blouse under the plane, and
honeysuckle sprouted from its skin.

Cut, Replace

Thomas Jefferson had a daughter
Lucy Elizabeth (1780–1781) and
then had a daughter Lucy
Elizabeth (1782–1784), which maybe
made mourning more efficient, like

a corset. Who can blame
him? If you had an
ox fall into a pit
wouldn't you pull it back
out again? My college boyfriend

broke up with me because
I kept calling out the
wrong name. Once I called
my cat. I was confused.
In the Bible two disciples

were named James which made
one The Less. I don't
even like my own name
because it sounds like a
nerd's, you know, the way

one snotty girl ruins Annabelle
forever. Jefferson made his own
Bible, cut out litanies of
so-and-so begat so-
and-so and even the

parts where the children were
raised from the dead and

he didn't replace them with
anything. It became a slim
volume. I thought the little

neighbor boy said it was
a baby tree in his
front yard but it was
The Baby Tree planted when
his little brother died. When

you say useless sorry words
so many times, you wish
you could cut them out
of your tongue. The tree
is a crabapple. I don't

care about its long scientific
name or how many sparrows
are making nests: after the
birds take wing and every
rotten apple falls, we will

have to chop it down.

Search Party, Called Off

There are lakes so big
they can swallow planes whole,
leaving behind no evidence, no bones
scattered at the mouth of a cave.
There's something nice about one body
being contained perfectly within another,
though the mourning family reminds us
it's the lake that's to be envied and not
what's lost inside. Still, nesting dolls.
X marks the spot. I was convinced
when I was a child that a board I found
embedded in the backyard was the lid
of a box containing the most precious
thing I could think of: a baby, quiet and
somehow alive, and when I shoveled it out,
its eyes would blink open in sunlight,
its tiny fists close and unclose
as if being discovered for the first time
in my arms. I didn't worry that the earth
would mind being left with such a gap.
Eventually it would smooth over
with dirt and water, and something
would take hold and bloom.

Notes

"Ice Cave: Shoshone, Idaho" draws language from "Shoshone Ice Caves" Field Review at RoadsideAmerica.com and trial coverage from the *Times-News Magic Valley*.

"Infinite, Separate Houses" takes its title from Whitman.

"Sweet and Golden Soup" uses information from "398. Bridge to Nowhere: A Map of Golden Gate Jumpers" on StrangeMaps. Wordpress.com, which is curated by Frank Jacobs.

"Preordained" owes an image to Amanda M. Burgess.

"Dust Bowl, 1936" references imagery in Pare Lorentz's documentary *The Plow That Broke the Plains* (1936) and Ken Burns' *The Dust Bowl* (2012).

About the Author

Bethany Schultz Hurst's poems have appeared in *Cimarron Review*, *Crab Orchard Review*, *The Gettysburg Review*, *River Styx*, *Sixth Finch*, and other journals. She holds an MFA from Eastern Washington University. She lives in Pocatello, Idaho, with her husband and son, and teaches creative writing at Idaho State University.